MILLENNIAL F.

By the same author

The Cost of Seriousness (1978; reissued in Oxford Poets 1987)
Collected Poems (1983; reissued in Oxford Poets 1988)
Fast Forward (1984)
The Automatic Oracle (1987)
A Porter Selected (1989)
Possible Worlds (1989)
The Chair of Babel (1992)

MILLENNIAL FABLES

Peter Porter

Oxford   Melbourne

OXFORD UNIVERSITY PRESS

1994

Oxford University Press, Walton Street, Oxford OX2 6DP

Oxford New York Toronto
Delhi Bombay Calcutta Madras Karachi
Kuala Lumpur Singapore Hong Kong Tokyo
Nairobi Dar es Salaam Cape Town
Melbourne Auckland Madrid
and associated companies in
Berlin Ibadan

Oxford is a trade mark of Oxford University Press

First published in Oxford Poets
as an Oxford University Press paperback 1994

British Library Cataloguing in Publication Data
Data available

Library of Congress Cataloging in Publication Data
Porter, Peter
Millennial fables / Peter Porter.
p.   cm.—(Oxford poets)
I. Title, II. Series.
PR9619.3.P57M55 1994 821—dc20 94–9234
ISBN 0–19–282391–4

1 3 5 7 9 10 8 6 4 2

Typeset by Rowland Phototypesetting Ltd, Bury St Edmunds, Suffolk
Printed in Hong Kong

For William Trevor

ACKNOWLEDGEMENTS

Acknowledgements are due to the editors of the following periodicals and newspapers in which some of these poems first appeared: *Acumen, Adelaide Review, Ambit, Blue Nose Poetry Anthology, London Review of Books, The Printer's Devil, Poetry and Audience, Poetry Book Society Supplement 1993, Poetry Review, Rencontres Poétiques en Suisse Romande, Salt, Scripsi, Sunday Times, The Times, The Times Literary Supplement, Voices*.

One poem, 'Serenade' was included in *Barry Humphries: Reappraisements on his Birthday*. Several poems were printed in the limited edition pamphlet, *Sixes and Sevens*, published by Folio (Western Australia).

The author would like to thank the Literature Board of The Australia Council for giving him a Category A Fellowship at the beginning of 1994 which enabled this collection of poems to be produced on schedule, and will further assist him in devoting time to poetry in the future.

CONTENTS

The best in this kind are but shadows, and the worst are no worse, if imagination amend them.

A Midsummer Night's Dream, v:i

I

THE APPROACH ROAD

They didn't tell you how you were to go,
Only that you must start and having started
Should keep in mind the big road up ahead,
That what you swore to do as you departed
Would be forgotten in the contraflow
Of signs you followed, skirmishes you led
While wilful herds went slow and insects darted.

The twilight thickens and the darkening road
Appears to narrow through its banks of green;
The clouds and trees have fossilized together
As if they wouldn't let the car between—
Here are the megaliths the route-map showed,
The dried-up lake, the starveling moor of heather,
Yourself the image on the startled screen.

FORTY YEARS ON

It was notation of the English air
which brought me here
that blood not words in books might share
with me this working hemisphere.

Which brought me here,
hope or despair? I knew I took
with me this working hemisphere.
What was inside the final book,

hope or despair? I knew I took
a step which could not be retraced.
What was inside the final book
if it were shown must be outfaced.

A step which could not be retraced,
(it was notation of the English air),
if it were shown must be outfaced
that blood not words in books might share.

LITTORAL TRUTH

You are discovering one of the mimetic truths
About Australia—it is a long and silver littoral
Within the sound of surf, a country rhymed by waves
And scanned by the shifting outlines of the bay.
We are all still strangers on its shore—the palms,
The Norfolk pines, the painted face of concrete to the sea—
No matter how far from the coast you go you only
Leave yourself and drift in double legend to
An old impossibility—no wonder those explorers sought
An Inland Sea; it was the pool of madness in them
Fed by rivers running into nothing. Relax instead
Along the endless shore, the mountain seas of sand,
The various heads and raging bars where change of tide
Rips channels to a narrow bottleneck—you can be
Odysseus or Captain Cook, forget the package tours
Flying into Cairns, the washed-up stubbies on the beach,
And step into a balanced darkness, mangroves, mud
And soft withdrawal at late evening. Your inheritance
Is welcoming you, and as you flap along the sandbanks
Look out to sea and watch the tourist preen himself:
'Thus sung they in th' Australian boat' but not to praise
The land, themselves or God, but with a level voice
To mark their presence in a sky of perfect stars.

THE PICTURE OF LITTLE P.P. IN A
PROSPECT OF PHOTOGRAPHERS' PROPS

See on this oval stained by time
A burial's beginning smiles
As last makes first its paradigm.
Here childhood's milky background teems
With brightness rushing out of dreams
And guileless charm itself beguiles:
              The photograph
Shows 'Eden 1930', minus staff.

A middle-class concern looks out
From coloured cheeks and tousled hair
And carefully modulated pout.
This Darling of the Gods is sure
Of nothing but there must be more
To love than his allotted share:
              Between his knees
The world, a coloured ball, is held with ease.

His two fists like two running shafts
Stretch out to greet the tug of life;
His feet are well-tried rubber rafts
On which he'll float till out of sight
He rides the waves of lurid night—
Inside his head desire is rife:
              The tinter's hand
Has lightly coloured all the seeming sand.

This studio's the world at large
Where decades of the worst which man
Can do are immanent: the barge
He sits in burns on mystic waters,
A scion of transplanted Porters
He stays as distant as Japan:
              The marvel is,
Of democratic riches, all are his.

Time which lingered in the shutter
Has wound a universe since then
On yearly reels, yet puerile stutter,
The prelude to full-grown despair,
Seems still to haunt the pictured air
And apprehension broods again:
                    The only child
Is cramming all disguises in one smile.

CONNECT ONLY

I'm drinking illicitly
from a bathroom mug
in a Writers' Retreat
some Montepulciano d'Abruzzo,
not my favourite wine
but usually the one
inside those carrier-bags
sold on Italian stations
to hungry travellers,
and I am back again
with a pretty companion
I don't get on with sharing
lunch en route to Ferrara
where we won't sleep together
and I'm happy to allow
this memory of the train
to remind me of the time
my wife and I encountered
a man who entered our carriage
at Padua and masturbated
against her thigh all the way
to Venice, and I wouldn't
say anything to stop him
out of embarrassment
and he justified me
by pointing beyond the causeway
and welcoming us—'Eccola
Venezia'. A simpleton,
he more or less resembled
a beautiful Renaissance male
in a portrait on a postcard,
and my wife is dead and she
didn't resent what he did,
only my cowardice, and I
need forgiveness of them both
which is why that postcard
is ample occasion and reason
for my mind to wander to
other postcards and other

parts of Italy and on to days
before we went from England
for our holidays and the kids
were tucked up for the night
and we'd sneak out to find
a pub and look to see if each
could somehow find the key
to the other's doubtful heart
and failed, I'm sure, but still
felt closer for the try,
yet somehow this won't fix
and back comes drink, the days
of scouting bottles locked
in drawers of knickers or
stuffed behind old shoes,
the death watch born of life—
all this was years ago
but who believes in time
whose body bears him on
to where all memories meet
or has the style to face
the picture of himself
when wine must have a stop?
Now gadarene the words
run headlong down the page,
old symbols no one trusts—
alas, we're trained to tell
back to ourselves at night
the endless consequence
of being alive and hands
revelling in such trust
reach out as well they might
for wine in bottles rich
with the red threads of death.

NIL BY MOUTH

Life enters by the mouth and so that's closed
to all but air. High drips are spider-lines
to bring relief. How beautiful when young
these bodies were which now lie wrecked on sun-
framed catafalques. Life never ages and
the mind is breakfasting on horrors: it
saw death with death's permission, a tall screen
of glass on which was scripted a cascade
of algebraic formulae moving up
and down and from its inhumanity
evil shone in lights. This final change
revealed how life began on earth, a conflict
of prime numbers tending always to equate
to nothingness. But on these beds there lie
the casualties of that incarnation,
strange numériques engrossed by flatulence,
forensic tropes made man with catheters.
If we were spirit only we would have
to burn all records, shun the eight o'clock
white-coated caravanserai and give
despair its due. Instead, we lucky ones
will soon go home—until one day ahead
a choking food will fill our open mouths
and scrutineers will take down warning signs,
the screens be drawn and loyal sun shut out.
Ask the chaplain what he always says:
'Language is the only thing which we
possess at death we didn't have when born.'
These buildings rose to audit any gain.

COVENT GARDEN IN THE SIXTIES

Here where bridges to the past
may be trodden by a team of cheating gods
or carry the companionable dead
back to life from their long overcast
empyrean, we sat, not quite at odds
with one another, staring ahead
at the usual muddle on the stage.
Maestro Solti's dome, tympanum
of a Straussian downbeat, bobbed
above the pit. Two ladies of uncertain age,
tiara'd, satin'd, shifted bum to bum
through three long acts, happily hob-nobbed
with their kind in intervals
and made our evening comic at the end—
one asked, 'What did you make of it?'
'Too long, too loud.' That memory annuls
for me the real pain the music sends
straight to my slow conscience: I admit
that marriage and the seed of life need Strauss
to fill them with appropriate harmony.
Human creatures worsen in the light
and cannot make a temple of a house;
the birds which clamour in the family tree
are vultures and not falcons; every night
the court of dreams must pass its sentence
while scores and books and pictures rush
to judgment on their makers—why else
come where the trials of gods commence,
where Neo-Babylonian tiers of plush
pretend they wait on pleasure and our hells
and heavens are strictest shuntings of the air.
I know we courted love and couldn't believe
that it had come and then that it had gone—
years later in a park I saw a pair
of birds like us—she streamed, he had to weave,
hopalong goose who thought himself a swan.

TOGETHER AGAIN

I was strangely back—here, there or somewhere—
And these were my old friends talking at lunch
And he who was dead was brilliant, his hair
Never grey its full chestnut again. The crunch
They were saying, when it comes to it, is who
Outside his body can be sure of his work
Or companionship? Not so, I thought, this too
Is involuntary, each dream is a perk
Of the moment's perfection: this unity
Is waiting in time and compels us forever.
Then they were gone but one voice said 'See,
Our reunion's as unsure as the weather,
As slippery as dreams always are—for instance,
You thought that our dead friend was happy,
But he came on parole that terrible distance
Out of their custody, Time's KGB—
"Nightmare Shepherds" he called them, the ever-grim
Shadows he'd borne in his blood, and rather
Than fail us had let them arraign him—
Poor ghost of a son, despising his father.'

SERENADE

In manner of a mystery we hear
in one man's choice of notes played then by trained
musicians complex valencies of ear.

So in unfairness fairness is explained;
that beauty should be felt the felt is hailed
and all are gainers by desire detained.

If changing of desire to action failed
just once, a million times or sometimes never,
potentiality was yet regaled.

Each night the dreaming self has sought to sever
all lines to consequence, but dawn proposes
a serenade both opulent and clever.

We all own shares in what one mind composes;
it is our nerves which temper the full scale
and ours the compromise its passion glozes.

That human chances, like the working snail,
live in a house of slowness is a fix
on fruitfulness, a halo of detail.

And music, that most serious of tricks,
puts on its wig to pose as justice here—
the gods give up their Zimmer-frames and sticks

And walk upon the waves in perfect fear.

LATE IN THE DAY

Following Yeats's *Cold Heaven* is nominal
Suicide, says the soul, always in its place
As careful accuser, sound as the Binomial
Theorem, waiting its call to the Palace.

Risktakers Anonymous meets on this page.
If you speak up you may find your words
Opposed to your desire, taking it down a peg,
Still wielding archaic symbols like the sword.

So sort out eternity on the retina,
Try to see what Yeats saw through marine
Astigmatism in Ravenna, retsina
Made old Chian, Lowell lapped in Maine.

The hemstitching to God, an eyes-down draw
Where any word may fill the card: our pens
Drip with effrontery as we edge toward
The Grail—inside its lip, EPNS.

Late in the day of language, life below
Is blocked by souls thick as cloud on Carmel,
Resented by the living who must bellow
At a Heaven cooked to caramel.

HAPPINESS

The world's a window on to death
With killers closing in to kill,
But love of life's a shameless zest
    Persisting still.

The sun eclipsed by passing cloud,
The icicle upon the sill,
With feeling in their gift were proud
    Of standing still.

To have survived another night
Is all the pelting bloodstream's skill
And purpose through the octave's height
    Sounds surely still.

Our language lacks George Herbert's nerve,
His more can only make ours less,
And yet we cross his lines and swerve
    To happiness.

SIXES AND SEVENS

Of equilibrium
the spirit must speak as of the blood's once garden
before leaves fell on the blackened sundial
and loquacious floribunda stood trial
by tempest: then pardon
was for the ugly bug at the very brim
of existence,
born judge of distance.

Ur-chaos, disorder
and the innumerate span of the warm bird-table
was a nescience needing to be tamed
in a republic of nerves: so they blamed
the set gods of Babel
who must be acknowledged at the border—
of course these were
the ten digits of fear.

Ever-smooth decimals
though not asked to be widely or crudely divisible
unlike their harrowing neighbours followed
a strictly formulaic code
and being biddable
took then to the policing of cells,
their cold heavens
at sixes and sevens.

Achieving due balance
consequently required a lunatic proportion
which right thinkers consider tragic,
not science nor philosophy, but magic,
as on the gold valance
of Alcalá de Henares height's tortion
keeps protesting
at two storks nesting.

ESTATES AND SUNSHINE

And the poet stressed the flies. Metaphorical flies,
But we have real ones settling and rising
From curled-up sheets of veal, their noses pressed
Against the windows of the restaurants
With punning names, and sheets of sunshine
Unexpectedly on dried-up river courses
Where the birds, unlike the cattle, cannot vote,
The SAS at practice by the largest broiler-farm
Before the Marches, then an industry of piano-legs—
It's keeping-on, it's Heritage, survival,
Heartbeat of the flags, and what could satire do
Against the need to live? It would say the world
Is glorious to its summer friends and spends
The substance of its titlement to make a show
For privilege to sprawl in, coaxing
Glottal shifts from Underclass to Underpass.

The writer throws his hands up in despair
And gives his vote once more to saintly Herbert.
Here's beautiful thought immaculately engraved
And God Himself in all His jerseys playing.
Perhaps we should conclude that writing verse
Is gas and water, little bits of good concluding
In depressed assessments while unfairness
Hits the fan. After Adam, only an evolution
Nobody believes in could alter things, and death
Attending patiently is the single democrat in sight.
Go for the round journey, travelling against the sun—
There may be somewhere favoured by true progress—
Finding it will put you in the corner-seats of boats
Or ordering coffee in uncleaned Transit Lounges
Remembering the pilgrim's modern text:
I to A, 'We're off again.' A to I, 'Oh, goody!'

INTO THE GARDEN
WITH THE WRONG SECATEURS

The soul requires a second for repentance.
An afternoon can seem eternity.

The Open Verdict or The Open Way,
each leading to the unrevolving door . . .

The Press reports Police recruiting's up,
the crime statistics are encouraging.

Bring back internment for our terrorists,
imprison them in decent people's thoughts.

Lifting the vagrants in the park to gaze
across the reins of Elijah's chariot . . .

Spring tides bring duckboards to the Square,
new ways to rout the sickly pigeons.

The gorilla agrees to masturbate more often
to encourage visitors and save the Zoo.

Courtesy of a top team of researchers
this virus enjoys a photo opportunity.

The Government rebukes those cynics who
doubt the range of choice in its Rapist's Charter.

Psyche was consumed by revelation
but caught a glimpse of dirty pants.

Because you can't make your poems modern
don't say Shakespeare found it just as hard.

Since privatization of the means to fame
Post-Modernist thugs control the Book Reviews.

We who hate metrication still agree
the working syllables be fixed at ten.

The Party's manifesto promises support
for elfin epics as well as villanelles.

The angel who appeared to Constantine
was doing PR for a new anthology.

Trapped in their fortress by unlettered troops
the Imperial Army lived on epigrams.

Sin is content to work for very little
but Virtue insists on a minimum wage.

Theory One: we need language to invent *King Lear*.
Theory Two: we need *King Lear* to invent language.

Hier ist kein warum.
Ne pas chercher à comprendre.

NOT THE THING ITSELF
BUT IDEAS ABOUT IT

It wasn't the blackbird at the window
but the colourless bird inside his sleep
which he could hear. It was saying nothing
about the world the blackbird praised
and nothing about a God among the pillows.
And so it had an end-stopped beauty,
being sheer idea, however redundant
to imagination. Something in him said
there is no new knowledge of reality,
just the idea of self still hovering
above each thing, a halo borrowed from
masters who believe in what they see.

ADDRESS TO THE STARS

These points of light which metaphors debate
Disclose a separation so extreme
Infinity awakens from its dream,
A tongue-tied horizontal figure eight.

Since they are unimaginable, we
Invert them till they shine through inner space:
Up close they act as gods whose laws replace
Extrapolation with sublimity.

O stars encompassed by our measurements,
Your integers show where belief may build
And adding noughts until the chart is filled
Exchange eternity for immanence.

A GEORGE HERBERT WORD GAME

So this contestant, ever keen to win,
   Seeks the big prize, his name in newspapers;
He's come to the bright studio, opinion.
    And looks through light at ranks of seated gapers
    And names his first word speedily—CONTRIVANCE.

The odds are gathered and the Quiz Master,
   Whose glowing jowls no cynicism shades
And whose dress suit is holy alabaster,
    Double-pumps his jet of accolades
    And cheers another win—SINCERITY.

To go for broke the highest word is sought.
   In Durables brief fame is soon consumed
Though to the cheque they add another nought—
    Blame each of us in whom the world is doomed,
    We all contest a golden NATURALNESS.

    CONTRIVANCE is CORRUPTION in advance,
    SINCERITY is SIGNING what you see,
    NATURALNESS is NOTHING more or less.

WE 'SEE' HIS POEMS WITH
A THRILLING FRESHNESS

What do we see
when we read 'his' poems?
We are encouraged to leave the page.

A boy in an ironbound boarding-house
reads a book about Dragut the Corsair—
he is lounging on a candlewick bedspread.

He is not coursing through the famished roads
beyond St Elmo. He is seeing, so to say,
inside quotation marks.

'We too make noises when we laugh or weep.'
Now the quotation marks
are a gesture towards copyright.

'The physical world' too is a phrase
most of us knew before we discovered
it belonged to Wallace Stevens.

It was part of our first great poverty,
after which we met one greater,
the rational poverty of poetry.

Instead, this exercise in sound: C,
The Good Shepherd, is translated to the See
of York, from which you cannot see the sea.

WORLD POETRY CONFERENCE
WELCOME POEM

Brothers and sisters, whether joined or singlish,
    We bring you greetings from our lovely land—
Everything will be exposed in English
    so delegates and lovers understand.

We are in no doubt publishers of Man
    and Man has thieved the spark which fires the clay,
so welcome everyone and sparkle soon
    and we will have for certain a nice day.

Our country has great dams and several sorts
    of mentionable fruit—what has yours?
Our friendly poems like to go in shorts
    and your hotel will have the cricket scores.

What do we need with Scuds and Dreadnothings
    when smart's the word for pantoums and haiku?
Our Minister has made war so disgusting
    that we love peace and poetry like you.

We say our neighbours are the sun and moon
    and we make love to ocean with our feet.
We hope that you will couple with us soon
    to join our satisfactory élite.

A GADARENE PROJECTION

Between two pillars of the mind
   ten feet apart is where they shelter,
loudspeakers, humanly designed
   to make their air a sonic delta.

But these are markers of mere space
   to them—cats can unreel the distance
rolling past each loving face
   without the help of Brahms's pistons.

What has it done for them, this surge
   of music surfing in their hearing?
Theirs and the moral world might merge
   if seeming were more like appearing.

And then perhaps the notes would pump
   a blend of God and mathematics
through their veins and make them jump
   from flowered balconies and attics

with parts of us inside their heads,
   a truly Gadarene projection,
out of their calm and sultry beds
   with no consenting recollection

of feline meals and murders to
   abate their abstract apprehension,
a strange self-immolation due
   to J. S. Bach's Two-Part Inventions.

THE GOLDEN AGE OF CRITICISM

After so many crowded centuries
consumers have their say, with extra helpings
of old Gainsboroughs, recorded round-ups
of an epoch's tabulature. There in a pale
among the factories of Arcadia some are working
at packing time into its crates of knowledge
(rather like binding children's feet or getting
Paradise Lost by heart). They have staunched
the flow of the Castalian tap and now
put down their heavy wrenches: they are happy
saying of Sylvia she paid a higher price
to the Ferryman, or of Sam he made the sun
stop above a cemetery. We play
at their feet, our timeless childish shouts
reminding them of filing systems and
the supernatural codings. Suddenly
they see, on the Grammarian's height,
just what serenity there is, a sort
of 'characteristic landskip' drawn
with the pencil of a Claude or Corot
and they know this is The Golden Age
of Criticism, and as darkness dawns
on the inverted sky they sing vesperal
hymns to old humanity, the gods
that rise in rivers, shepherds calling to
their flocks across a sculpted quadrangle.

STILL IT GOES ON

The numbers are such we cannot
    hope to evoke them,
all mankind rising to God,
    filling his cloakroom

And passing the door beyond death
    into full Judgement,
every wrong straightened out there,
    love all ungrudging.

But how can the creatures we are
    cease to be fallible?
Great crimes may be excused, yet
    self is indelible.

When mine and my rival's bones are
    unearthed together
our words will be mutually as
    hostile as ever.

ABOVE THE VILLA LINE

Importance grows sparsely at these heights
marked off from the valleys of trout farms
and geranium-flanked gardens
by several lines of concrete pylons
and their curving cables. Here, so far above,
the seekers after calibration come
to look down on the ranked achievements
noting nothing stays the same—a hairpin bend
is being widened, a new 'Caves' is opening
beside a family florist, and out of sight
beyond the row of trees now reaching heights
intended twenty years ago a truly monumental
half-palazzo wins the echo-prize of envy.
Yes, all is and must be well where time's
a neighbour and decay and growth are pairs
of equal opportunity, the modern gravamen.
Above the villa line live those who heard
the death-cry of success. They bring their hopes,
scenes poorly dressed and lacking all
equivalence: life is jumbled and its order
sheer occurrence. Charcoal-burners' huts
alternate with ragged radar-posts,
the grass imagines record frosts through
statutory summer and sheep slip down
to pasture by the drawling brook
if once the old dog turns his back. But we
are drawn to this imagined place—
here we may find the attributes
which furnish our desire to praise
(failure must sing as sweet an anthem
as success but cannot settle for
the lushness of a valley life)—
you find us now attempting monodies
to rival the *a capella* of the towns,
our ego-stained and envy-nurtured tunes
becoming lambent objectivity
while those who choose to leave on looking back
are graced to see a chute of fire descend
and stern observers turning into salt.

THE PAINTER OF THE PRESENT

Living in the present is well yes perhaps.
The present has a nasty attitude,
it reminds you that everyone's gone out
and left you all alone, that someone
on a bike's in danger on a crowded road,
that there are more snails drying in the sun
than could be saved by a rescue squad of Buddhas.

Which is why the past is more hospitable.
Say of this old castle scarcely visible
through the oleanders of the autostrada,
Castruccio erected it in 1423
and you cleanse it in an instant
of blood and history and even disinfect
the car of all the sulks of family outings.

But to be serious about both past and present
is another case. It strikes you suddenly
that reality has no style; to picture it
or represent it you will need a handle—
that's why you told that tense young man
that cadences from Bach won't work today
though every note he wrote is humming still.

So, contrive a style and let the subjects come.
Good Heavens, what a soiled and circumstantial
set of applicants! And how unworldly.
Last night I dreamed of being snubbed by one
I'd done great harm to. So I woke afraid.
But now my pen insists on frisking through
the drains of medieval Sinalunga.

No, not unworldly, just unserious.
The oilcloth on this table is itself,
my stomach is itself, but these my words
belong to no one, are on the coat of arms
of nowhere. Stevens had a window on to
Truth? Reality? . . . something anyway
his poems spoke for. Someone pushed it shut.

Putting his black cap on the Judge is sure
his words make proper sense. But the true tyrant
needs only a gesture or a change of smile,
his syllables unfolding in our screams.
And for a bonus let us now propose
two frightened enemies whose webs of hate
fill with the self-same flies of petulance.

The painter of the present lifts the shutters
from the window, opens his pattern book
(Leon Battista Alberti, courtesy of Phaidon)
and aided by despair takes up his brush
to claim the scene, and it can be the past,
the future, any platitude he likes,
but what he sees will change its blood in him.

UNSICHTBAR ABER SEHNSUCHTSVOLL

The record of one's wickedness, open before
The Almighty on the Bench, is not a book at all
but half a page torn from a scribbling pad—
worse, the police have hardly felt it necessary
to tamper with the evidence—
                          And a high waltzing
                          of the jargons beckons:
. The Left all documents and indignation,
The Right a tribal talk-back from the floggers'
triangle—
                          When the lambs are sprinkled
                          on the hillsides like silkworms
                          on their leaves and leaves themselves
                          have feather-soft pollution
                          on their undersides,
we are at the barricades of Middle-Time.
History has cleared the boulevards to ensure
the enfillade will cover every angle
and the Wizard waves his decimal-stark wand
to mark Millennium. Surprise reveals
that every old instruction is in place,
each dogma is as polished and restored
as some pre-war Bugatti and the phone-ins
fill with sing-song admonitions to espy
'a thousand years of rolling-back of Socialism'.
                          Our critics are so right—
                          we need a key to our emotions,
                          an algebra of art
                          which sounds the same
                          on any keyboard outing.
Why bother to be clever if your feelings work,
why not cry on cue (or cry at Kew)
and please the millions waiting to be pleased?
Soon they'll clear the files and publish every
crazy secret the Nomenklatura
kept of everybody.

                    At that time
                    (or at the hour of death)
you'll know what rings evasion's left
inside your heart and which of all the words
your feeling brought to mind still testify
                    beyond their written shape.

THE GRAND OLD TUNES OF LIBERALISM

They're the ones we never sang, we had it so good
but could always hear them through the decreed
miseries of classicism, the well-fee'd
alla marcias and symphonies of greed—
unheard melodies are sweeter, we understood.

All the great composers were heresiarchs
of happiness. They believed in it in notes
if not in lines, but a looking-out for votes
converted their long melodies to simple quotes
and Orpheus & Co's sound-bites in Sunday parks.

Just like the Church, the deeper thinkers held
that misery's modes and scales were Nature's voice
from the abyss, that modulation's choice
precluded choosing and equality was noise:
since Art was Fascist, Nature must be as well.

But yet the notes kept going cancrizans,
insisting on imbuing the human mind
with a glory it knew it left behind
in childhood—a sunburst for the blind
was the deaf composer's bequest to his fans.

It could never stay so even—back on earth
The Field of Folk turned out to be The Mob,
scholarship sat late assessing *Blow Job*,
an Epilion, and genius proved a snob—
everyone hummed the one tune from Perm to Perth.

Today we're trapped in faceless symmetry
as the white noise of Demos disputes air-time
with the monkish runes of Heritage, when chime
is held a wonder and accident a rhyme
and faction shouts beside the well-tempered sea.

Somewhere outlandish, perhaps above the blast
or more probably beneath it, a human sound
continues, pain and joy on common ground,
the Liberalism our fathers thought they'd found,
a bridge-passage to the future from the past.

They knew they were some kind of a solution
But wouldn't risk their legendary horses,
Battle wagons: they'd read about pollution,
High-rise slums and poisoned watercourses.

To keep their army healthy they ran races
On plains and let our cameramen record them—
Nightly the same professional drained faces
Fronted clips on TV and deplored them.

Their Great Khan broadcast from his tented city
His moderate ambitions while Supremos
Wrote for Sunday Papers and the witty
Juniors at the FO shredded memos.

This westward surge while seeming so dramatic
Required another horde pressing behind them.
Perhaps therefore our fear was automatic,
The need for devils showed us where to find them.

The Stock Exchange, the markets and the churches
Couldn't resist an 'après moi' prediction,
The think-tanks called for cross-the-board researches
And sad colloquiums defined our fiction.

Time might insist each was the other's Other,
The building-up and running-down of power,
But brother's empathy can offer brother
Only the fact of death and not its hour.

TRINACRIAN AETNA'S FLAMES
ASCEND NOT HIGHER

What sights the world has raised to soothe itself
 and filed away to serve as history
for its prophetic gift may still recur
 through blackened sands and obelisks of fire,
past cows like cut-outs of a *danse macabre*
 or well-oiled seabirds legless on the shore,
and fetch salutes from any public day,
 though sore despair, the wicked twin of self,
finds second options, settles down in towns
 with civic lakes and glassy streams for fate
to cast its sure and end-stopped lines into.

That's when the terror starts, when what's inside
 the mind exaggerates its syntax to
accommodate apocalypse—remember how
 one Sunday, pestered by the drizzle, you
sat on a beach whose windlass waves raised balls
 of shit along the promenade and where
behind your callow wincing flames climbed up
 the sky to paraphrase necessity—
lost and faceless in that stinging draught
 you narrowed God to make him fit The South
Durham Iron and Steel Company.

Just as the lines which grow now on the page
 espouse a hope that somewhere more complete
the ends of things make sense, that skies won't burn
 unless a saint is rising in his glory
or new volcanoes promise wonderland,
 so too transfiguration must expect
to turn the other cheek and do without
 the perfect food of truth, living for love
of this one planet out of millions where
 ·unrest is drenched in feeling and you are
a witness to the courtesies of fire.

INTENTS AND PURPOSES

We are the sifters of the language soup,
We see a straight line where you see a loop,
    And we can make
    Finnegan's Wake
As plain as Admiral Nelson on the poop!

We know that life makes sense, that every art
Is out to complicate the human heart—
    Bored by the real
    Art must conceal
That Stendhal was a cut-price Bonaparte!

Is all good structure in a winding stair?
Why climb Mt Everest? Because it's there.
    Your loyal computer
    Your only tutor,
Switch on! None but the brave deserve the fair!

So huge an apparatus, but alas
We only need to cut a little grass—
    It fills the room
    With heavy gloom—
The Mind is overstructured for its task!

Grow old along with me. What's yet to be?
Get tenure in a University.
    Those writer chaps
    Have need of maps
Like Beerbohm's Henry James down on one knee!

That language is subversive Judges know,
With *quis custodiet* their *quid pro quo*:
    Your Father's late
    But just you wait,
When he gets home the tears will start to flow!

The best lack all conviction while the worst . . .
Our Leader–Writer's angry, fit to burst,
      His certainty
      Conveys that he
Knows what the nation needs. (He got a First!)

Back in the rag-and-bone shop of the heart
The nucleus is split, things fall apart.
      Where chaos reigns
      There are no drains,
Love dies and Cressida's a high-class tart!

Minds swayed by eyes are full of turpitude.
The habit of quotation, we conclude
      Is just to show
      That here below
The screw that's turning is the turn that's screwed!

So come full circle, we're still on patrol.
We make you pay if your name's on the roll.
      We're always screening
      For lack of meaning;
Write what you like, but do as you are told!

To make our title good we speak TO ALL.
This electronic smog which fills the hall
      Won't go away,
      It's here to stay,
And Paradise once Lost taunts All That Fall!

GOES WITHOUT SAYING

Now why extend myself like this—
Of all the stanzas most remiss
When phrased in standard Englishes
        And not stout Doric
To choose that form which Burns made his,
        The catechoric!

I do it through perversity
To pay court to the arbitrary
Hoping unlike and like agree
        On skilful passes
As hurdling is the apogee
        Of sprints on grasses.

My theme is one which Burns could sell—
Waiting for Death or *Who Feels Well?*
But lacks the Calvinistic swell
        Which made his Ayrshire
As rich in hints of Heaven and Hell
        As ancient Persia.

And as my title brings to mind
A writer must use words to find
What should be wide and well-assigned,
        Extinction's riches,
Not just the blind leading the blind
        Plum into ditches.

But Breughel's picture tells a story
Too real to be an allegory:
Pain is life's hard territory
        And no mere word
Can stifle with a category
        What has occurred.

And yet we say it, paint it, sing it
And pay a thousand priests to bring it
(To quote from Hardy) and our wingèd
        Lauds and Complines
Flap on as worriedly as singlets
        On washing lines.

We should use terror to defuse
The bomb in us that's always news,
'That we'll lose all there is to lose',
                And consecrate
To death the power to lead as Muse
                Its other eight.

This must be how the world has seen
Amid injustice, cruelty, spleen,
The Queen of Heaven and the Queen
                Of darkest Diss—
True twins of love though neither keen
                On promises.

Because when we have passed away
They too will have nowhere to stay
They'll lend their prowess and obey
                The rules of art
Which while the body's bits decay
                Sustain the heart.

It's up to us then to invent
A place where beauty's consequent,
An Eden of the Immanent,
                Nature *en suite*
Where past and future strangely blent
                Repeat, repeat.

We have some instances of this
Compulsive metamorphosis
As first and last consent to kiss—
                Profound pre-echo—
And Birth and Death accept in bliss
                The same Art-Deco.

We wonder which rule will apply,
Transfiguration or blank sky?
But Richard Strauss took dying's cry
                And quickly froze it.
Death was just, when he came to die,
                As he'd composed it.

HUDIBRASTICS IN A HURRY

If only my poetic slot
Like Pope's to Dr Arbuthnot
Might scold in so abrupt a wise
Its later urge to catechise
Should be forgotten in the jar
Of my superb vernacular,
My 'bar the door', 'turn up the Telly'
Smack properly of Machiavelli
And not be just a desperate hope
To fit millennial shades on Pope.
To plunge in Hudibrastics is
The only way to make them fizz
But when the masters set them going
They could expect no reader's slowing
Down since indignation then
Was poised on each poetic pen
And relished at enormous length
By connoisseurs of satire's strength—
It's doubtful if they thought reform
Would be the outcome—but the norm
Was biting, wounding without quarter
(Distortions faced by their distorter!),
A curious consensus that
The thin might prosecute the fat
For moral self-indulgence while
The fat in just as sure a style
Damn as politically correct
All members of the skinny sect—
So politics and satire screen
The simple things we really mean
When wrapped in indignation our
Blame's as righteous as it's sour:
We couldn't hate the fault if we
Hadn't first loathed the he or she
We castigate it in; a tort
Is little more than afterthought—
A shape of mouth, a cast of eye,
An uncleaned shoe, want of a tie,
Too loud a voice, too big a car,
Injustice of things as they are,

The world proved wrong inside a minute
Having such paranoia in it:
Thus huge moralities may be
Constructed on mere enmity,
Theologies of punishment
Brought down to squalls of rates and rent
With Janus-like the hates we had
Polemicised as good or bad.
The satirist is hired alas
To hide this truth and hold a glass
Up to Nature, warts and all,
Outside the plastic surgeon's stall
And with anathema instruct
The scalpel where to make a tuck.
Would it were so, that what we read
Were not diversion but a creed
And wicked-doers skewered by words,
Paleo-Gadarene, in herds,
Gave up their vices to confess
We'd saved them from the precipice,
But all along our pious urge
Is just where interest meets the verge
Of self and self's imperial thrust
(Oh for one friend whom you can trust),
All stoked by sullen entropy
And published as morality.
At last admit that satire's bite
Is germane to The School of Night,
A version of cold pastoral
Where simper is replaced by snarl,
Composed by everyone but Germans
And like Savonarola's sermons
As much to heat its own position
As to lead on to Inquisition
Though ending up, intent or not,
Insisting deviants be shot.
Must then all wringing of the withers
Or grading by didactic sievers,
High stamping on the moral ground,
J'accuse etc. be mere sound,

A recognition that the norm
Departed from gives us a form
To dress our crude ambition in?
To run the gauntlet of man's sin
We build a violent edifice,
A Souk of Wickedness and quiz
When its sad cast is long since dead
The reason why the work's still read,
Its annotated lines debated
And iconography collated—
The hard conclusion must be reached
That art is indignation bleached,
And urgent works of edification
Survive as texts in education,
The only use of their philippics
Tone registers and style specifics,
And when we judge them years after
Hear Swift through unembarrassed laughter
Declare with pride what genius
He had in youth when he wrote this.
The problem will not go away;
We must believe that what we say
Can change the world to some degree—
To halt the felling of a tree
Or topple some outrageous bully
Or work like Herbert's pious pulley—
But Auden warns us what he wrote
Hardly rocked the Nazi's boat
And things he told us we should do
Failed to save a single Jew.
Of course not! But we might examine
Not how best check Idi Amin
But test that other Auden maxim,
Committed poetry which packs 'em
Into sites of True Correctness
Or self-identified Electness
Will only draw attention to
The poet's own loud ballyhoo.
Unfair perhaps, but now recall
Those readings in our public halls

When bards would fight and scramble for
The chance to damn the Vietnam War—
Their reputations are intact,
Bank balances still in the black,
They've changed their brief to planet-saving
While ills of history like slaving
Are quite enough to damn a nation
In retrospective indignation,
And should good causes grow more scarce
There's internecine strife in verse
To keep their instant anger hotting
At names an epoch finds besotting—
Ho-Chi-min City *was* Saigon:
That cause is won—and they've moved on!
And yet this scorn may not be fair,
A writer cannot change the air,
He does no more than other men
When holding views and lifting pen
Or switching on his processor—
It's just that real events like war
Are hardly touched by authors' rage
In books, on TV or the stage;
Establishments for good or ill
Lick off the coating, spit the pill
But might as sop to probity
Dish out a bromide CBE.
The real danger's vanity—
Consider Yeats, a self-made stoic,
Who sneered at Owen's unheroic
Warning from the stinking trenches
That blood and pus and phosphorous drenches
Are not chivalric—this same Yeats
Posed high and mighty like The Fates:
'Did that play of mine send out
Certain men the English shot?'
And did it? Writers should reflect
That in the war with intellect
Emotion holds the highest cards
But more importantly by yards

The words we wrap emotion in
Like those our intellect finds kin
Are forged in every human heart
And don't need priming by high art.
The awful vanity of writers
(The grown-up fruit of nail-biters)
Is forgiveable perhaps
Since, of all men's, their inner maps
Show most that dragon-haunted Terra
Incognita, The Swamp of Error
(And pity those who have to rhyme
In words employed time after time)—
There, from the first autistic shock
Till Domesday, lurks the dreaded block:
What shall I write? Who shall I blame?
Have I the courage to name names?
This Devil I met in the dark
Is he the genius of The Ark?
What of a world where seeming seems
Less present than the idlest dreams?
But simple torments hurt the most
When at a party your bland host
Asks 'Should I then have heard of you?'
Enough's enough—an end is due,
It's time to recognize this foray's
No TGV but mud-caked lorry,
That names like Butler, Pope and Swift
If claimed will get the shortest shrift—
I mustn't think that my iambics
Are biting satire or svelte tantrics,
But more resemble, when they bat well,
The lines of Mabel Lucie Atwell
Or doggerel on Birthday Cards:
Forgive us all, we headlong bards,
Whose inwardest investments are
To follow a deceitful star
And be brought face to face at last
With everything we thought was past
Only to find that memory
Recycles life perpetually.

MILLENNIAL ROCOCO

Snow hasn't fallen for three seasons
and The Amanuenses' Almanac continues to outsell
The Illustrated Biodiversity Handbook;
Despite its fattening on Access Television
The National Guilt proves hard to privatize—
it tours Georgian sites in the only Wellington
still flying; A Euro-Disney opera opens
the new season at Glyndebourne-in-Greenland
(suggested evening dress, long sealskins
or Baffin Furs); 'Guess and Fear', the Kleinian
Aerobics Show, moves to Umbria for its
anniversary, 'What's the time, Mr Wolf?'
from every top piazza; A regulatory body, OFFSOD
is created to monitor the cost of Rent Boys
while the Eighty-Hour Week is made
a test case of Subsidiarity; A scientific team
working at composing new and individual words
for every number between infinity and nought,
reports it's reached one million, seven hundred
and thirty-seven thousand, nine hundred and eleven
(nothing to be published till the year 2000);
An outbreak of Mad Accountant's Disease
leads to the slaughter of every horse
in the racing stable of Sheikh Bin Liner;
Historians revising the Julian Calendar,
attempting to place Christ's birth at AD3,
are overruled by the UN Anniversaries Commission;
A computer virus which attacks only Shakespearean
commentaries is identified in thirty universities;
Language Poetry made from finest durium
is sold in Health Food Stores, with 'Animal
Crackers in My Soup' on permanent tape loop;
The Literary Cricket Match, 'Prefixes versus
Suffixes' fields a team of phone-in compères
against Harold Pinter's side of Marxist Millionaires;
The Philip Larkin Prize for Political Incorrectness
cannot be awarded as its judging panel—Amis,
Conquest, Worsthorne—are found dead in bed together—
'A Post Modern Mayerling' reads the headline

in The Guardian; Cunard embarks on building
'The Ruritania', its first cruise liner for a decade,
bringing work to a threatened shipyard
south of Oslo; 'Buns or Stutter', The Home Counties
Pop Group, stars at The Smithfield Show
and is pictured next to a forty hundredweight
stud Charolais; After a break-in at the Imperial
War Museum the following are found missing:
General Gordon's close-stool, Curzon's truss,
a sanitary towel of Nurse Cavell's and Churchill's
enema—'warped minds have done this' says
a spokesman for The Yard; The Millennial Census
reveals an excess of the Durationally-Privileged
over the Pristinely-Endowed leading to
a severe curtailment of state pensions;
Both the GLUT Trade Talks and The Level
Playing Field Inquiry Into Idiom break up
in fierce recrimination, and as usual
everyone blames the French; With attendants
dressed as gladiators and girl assistants
wearing badges announcing 'I'm Messalina,
what's your challenge?' the World's Largest
Sexual Emporium, 'The Old Porn Brokers',
opens in The Strand; In a world-wide hook-up
the BBC relays its ship's band still playing
on the quarterdeck of the *Titanic*, while
fish salute the Ensign in the dark.

II

HOMAGE TO ROBERT BROWNING

GIVE A DOG A NAME

And soft, two parents come
from luncheon to
a church athwart a stream
and notice as they pass
the ribboned weeds like eels
racing forever to the weir.

Treviso, San Francesco,
once an army commissariat,
restored to God and his free market
by the pious tourist trade.

Inside, two poets' children buried
with memorials appropriate
their fathers' names—
Pietro Alighieri and Francesca Petrarca,
still solemn in unversified content—
so long ago, we say, but fame
is not as brittle as loved bones.

Ourselves lost children
of a famous father,
we pray for peace as long
as Italy, for congruence
that's closer than a name.

AESOP'S DRESSING GOWN

The spillings on lapels and cuffs, according
to his fellow queuers at the bathroom door,
were sloppy eggs and greedy second helpings,
but he knew better—they were what healthy
overreachers of commercial mornings
make of conscience: he would study them
and see the fox and grapes, the farmyard shapes
these others never could construe. He fought
consensus with his smelly feet; if truth
came up as lumps it meant that lice
were called again to be inquisitors—
meanwhile that gravy stain should be
a pond for pompous frogs to trumpet in;
a crumb might make King Log but certainly
he'd blown his nose down one sleeve as King Stork.

What may an underdog perform if not
squeeze fables from occlusions of his brow?
Since Everyman is unreformable
he must be entertained with heavyweight
impactions of his own imagination.
Aesop set out for his appointment at
the portraitist's in his coat of many cringes,
more bad breakfasts than Achilles' shield
had ships and warriors, better shadows there
than death knew how to frame for underlings—
he might be thought when brash posterity
circuited the gallery some old
and grave retainer with a book, rather than
what he knew he was, a hired explainer
of the gods' obtuseness to the gods.

GUANO

'The man I call *The Sulky Sperm*
Still eats his garden dirt and drinks
His urine, yet from him I've learned
Just what Le Bon Dieu really thinks.
I curse this war. I'm in my prime.
Write soon, dear friend. We'll win this time.'

'My colleagues are all bigots; they
Oppose your theories since you're German:
I spent some hours yesterday
Searching *The Forsaken Merman*
For any signs of Transference—
Our country fights in self-defence.'

'The new act is superb, it's worthy
Of your immortal genius.
But send me more—I cannot see
For tears, and even set the Bus
Timetable in my haste tonight.
This stupid war upsets me quite.'

'My Estimable Colleague, I
Suggest with great respect that you
Temper your lofty spirit, high
And noble-souled, with that most true
And sane corollary, Good Taste.
The war? Call it Eugenic Waste.'

Islands where sea-birds nest high-steepled
Above the ocean become rich
In guano. Culture likewise is peopled
Layer by dead layer, the which
Say artists, selfish to the core,
Explains the altruism of war.

CLIVE AND OLIVE

Clive would close his eyelids lightly over his eyes,
increase the muscle pressure until patterned light
in broken colours came before his inner gaze,
everything growing brighter and changing shape
as he pressed still harder—this he called
his kaleidoscope of dreaming, knowing it to be
the land he'd come from through his mother's fluids,
loving it for being as infinite as space,
the only meaning he could give to death, his right
to move again across the screens of time. He'd stood
on that old verandah with its flapping booms and thought
of death. Death was a single piss and the biggest star
inside his head: it had a face which changed, a friend
suddenly both here and absent, a set of ordinances
for his father's bowels. And so Clive, whose
personality though noisy was quite mild,
invented Heaven and the future using anything
which came to hand, and had enough left over to make
Shoel and the latitudes of Hell. See him in his prime
at a console mounted in the stalls, three rows of seats
removed, levers to push back and dials to watch,
concentrating like a submarine commander
as the stage is filled with all Avernus' apes,
a boy in jeans mounted on a trumpet, a girl
with laminated legs astride a saxophone,
and music hanging loose from coigns of the baroque.
Thus Clive who'd go canoeing through his own bloodstream
worked the machines which reproduce the light
of self-immersion: for him the categories
smiled like wedding guests; God's love was digital
and when death came the only thing he'd need to do
was close his eyes again and put more pressure on
and enter childhood through a conflagration.

Olive was never certain where she was. Or who she was.
She could be cutting up her birthday cake, angling the knife
and dexterously rounding coloured ski-slopes, half-pink
marzipan and half-green wax, giving each applauding guest
a standing candle—she'd do this and then flee the room
to stare at rainclouds in the trees and have to be called back

to brave the party speeches: no one seemed to mind.
Olive was Clive's sister. She would stop a stranger
and ask him could he look down through her eyes at what
she knew was showing there—the dream she'd had last night
and couldn't now remember. Olive was informed by dreams
the world was her responsibility, and saving caterpillars
from the oleander might endanger it as much as any
of the forms of masturbation. Like Clive she trained
as a musician, but gave up cello to sing madrigals
because she liked the symbolism—'ah, then you die'
she'd cant in smirking phrases as she crushed the larvae
of the tiger moth. Yet still she couldn't say for sure
if she existed. She'd draw coordinates—her own trunk
stretched along the ground and set against a tree
which stood for God the Perpendicular—which only proved
that nothing of herself was there and no one could exist
even with some evidence. She hid beneath her parents' bed
when they were making love but soon fell fast asleep;
she left messages on answering machines: 'Remember
Metternich had never heard of Schubert; perhaps his secret
police hadn't done so either.' Olive grew old eccentrically
as ever, and woke each morning as God's sister,
a Feminist who'd cause him greater pain than brother
Satan. And when she fell, she knew she'd land at last
on a construction which would bear her weight,
a stave perhaps she might be printed on, the very
notes of consequence which had so far eluded her,
an everywhere somewhere on the chromatic scale.

Ambiguous dying was a way to stay alive
for exocentric Olive and impacted Clive.

HELPING THE POLICE WITH THEIR ENQUIRIES

Could the verandah have been so wide,
the boards so rotten and for God's sake
whatever happened to the two-stringed hammock?
How back-to-front my childhood was:
a house surrounded by roofed openness,
the cluttered darkness like a keep within—
other people had their flowered atriums
and benison of moons;
they lived in different ports where ships
were bees among the stiffened derricks
not our sand-fly niggardliness of masts
and stories reaching town too late
to magnify the equipoise of books.

Back-to-front but never upside-down!
I didn't think there was an orthodoxy
of time and season; I lived in a climate
of staged paper where without experience
knowledgeable dreams spoke with the force
of ideal parents. They said, as if they'd guessed
I'd settle down in poetry, one never should
look back, speed was the thing, the mind must skate
above its deadly pool—they saw the frowns
of critics and knew that love and comedy
retreated from such phantoms; they used up
light and sinew to sit down at last
in grooves created by their commonplace.
And there before I learned to read
I saw the endless volumes truth has bound,
its glitz gestalt, the rainbow-bridge of self
spanning an abyss of consciousness.

Good God, this is romantic. But what
can any human mind be conscious of
beyond its being there? Fear is the cousin
you remember best, your hard headmaster
with the change of clothes. The river banks
pile up with debris, there have been such floods
the landscape looks like mining on the moon,
yet just as you are handing out medallions

64

courtesy the Overseas Explorers' League
that horde of ancient haunters bounces in
hallooing passwords and old College Songs—
girl-friends, women you could not unscramble
from the Lovers' Decalogue, tread this ground
with no need of permission: somehow they fit
coordinates, even the darkened parts
of childhood—each loving presence though it lied
desires your good and nestles up to you,
completely sexual but chaste with tears—
they wear the uniform of Hermes and one
will take you off on that official ride
where all the verbs are running, life's analogue.
Knowing the dream will fade you say to your
custodians behind the scene, 'We're all friends here,
we're helping the police with their enquiries.'

THE WORST INN'S WORST ROOM

You face it now with terror, but it seemed
while still far off a simplification
devoutly to be wished, a happy tugging
at the curtain of the airless archive room,
not wondering or caring what the sun might make
of such empowering.
                    Immediately, lights
go on in snappy phrases: *descensus Averno*
says the dust which every printed letter makes;
nothing will be wasted in this palimpsest
of penetration; forgiveness even
must be looked up in the Grand Concordance
while Paranoia's name-tapes are unstitched
from mass psychology and none can tell
whether *terra clausa* is the anus or
the painted desert.
                    Perverse remembrance
trying to account for dreams of cruisers
and Zapata-like assassinations
can do no better than assume you know
what Anne, Countess of Winchelsea,
wrought on her napery.
                    'In fading silks compose
faintly the inimitable rose.'
                    When Bougainville
brought Aotourou to Versailles from
his South Seas expedition, he gave a boost
to ballet, and the native, growing rich and fat,
died in Mauritius going home. I could
have made it Bennelong but as they say
what a gain for gourmet cooking if
the French not the British had settled
in Australia. Yet, on the other hand,
what a loss to ballad-writing.
                    Thus far unable
to make progress with what's serious
and must come soon, this calculation
moves to another page as if the world
were in a book and now at last the final
chapters were in sight. Age and health

are not the issue—just intertextuality.
Finest dislocations of the avant-garde
turn out to be the simplest captions of
disease and the pocket-book of dreams
is all that's left when fire destroys the libraries.
            And we emerge
like bomb-disposal experts in the ruins,
tapping at a drawer of microfiches,
decoding lettering on toasted calf—
'Through Borneo on a Penny-Farthing',
'The 218 Plots of Kotzebue',
'Function and Disfunction in Amnesia'—
and suddenly it seems so beautiful,
printing's aural mysticism,
a low sea-wall of objectivity
against whose groynes time surges every day
until a smothering subjectiveness
overwhelms the sky.
                Meanwhile a god has landed—
stepping out of Auden's borrowed craft,
he dries his wings and trills his generalities
in proper Viennese:
                'Du schöner stiller Gott'—
your dust is dancing in the final beams
declining from the uncleaned windows—you
compose the patient on the bed with stars
inside his eyes, the barque of Pharaoh warping
to his side and chroniclers on hand—
time to forget all childhood mysteries
and dotages; each pronoun must renounce
its birthright and the catechism start
with namelessness, alarm and ecstasy.

From THE MARIA BARBARA NOTEBOOK

. . . I cannot understand
how, like the ease and precision with which
he puts his notes on paper and boxes their ears
when choirboys turn them into travesties
of music, we are so very numerous
and yet so solitary—the one,
the self, the single, a paralysis of numbers,
the pain of ending at our fingers' ends!
I am an accumulation of particles
but have to be a system emulating
death's preferred design. To be caught
apprehending like Prometheus
a veiled intention, one hand on the rock,
stealing a little fire scarcely enough
to warm a lying-in—there you have it,
woman's part in creativity—
he couldn't get his sounds if getting lives
were not both pious and responsible,
a tempering of the not-yet-perfect scales
of love. And so I write down in this book
the trivia he sprinkles on the day
as if he's watering an office plant
in bureaucratic sunshine. The little gigues,
musettes and cats' cantatas emulate
the great phantasm of Jesus trapped in words
while out of sight hooves of the Lutheran
Cavalry ring their deliverance on
our Sunday faces. Where does he get such texts?
—the howls of sin, whispers of repentance,
Jordan stealing through the banks of truth,
an oboe's outline like a planet in
the dark, the camels in C Major to
their hocks. I see a stranger in the house,
a person from Pforzheim come to call
with some unmeaning message—several times
today I've met him in the hall. Dark angel,
what will become of us when the music
has to stop? Strange that everything seems used,
familiar from some other life, perhaps
before or even after this: my children

climb the hill to peer in at the Crib
like junior Magi and I hear the horns again,
the rolling 12/8 caravan of God.
Take me Lord when this life is complete.

. . . and yet I cannot go
when this bewildered air is beating with
the wings of children. That's my firstborn son
at the harpsichord learning disappointment
and an aptitude for drinking. I fear for him,
I fear for me. 'Before Thy Throne I stand
at last.' But who may abide the hour of our coming?
There's one who may, for whom the city slates
are pedals of an everlasting glory,
whose trees are rushing in discursive quavers
over printed graves: he faces both
the end and the beginning, cadence of
our purposes on earth—how glorious
the work he does, how impulsively his health
is measuring out my death. He'll remarry
and the published world renew its catalogue
of wonders: choirboys will hang on notes
like bells when my Exequien is rung,
the trumpeters be changed to dovelike
cooings of despair and memory unhinge
the darkened windows of our afternoons.
Ah, such fatal fluency—another
foray into F Minor—Friedemann
has all his father's skill except his love
of God. How long a road we tread and yet
we always wish it longer. Now a fugue
in three parts with a tortuous subject
and overcast by dissonance. The garden
fills with rain but through its veil I see
the shapes which come to tell me I must leave.
They urge me like a child to say my prayers.

. . . our cat has dribbled on
a hassock I'd brought home from church to mend—
I'll stitch it when it dries. I dreamed
God's tongue was licking me as I sat through

a sermon catatonic with theology,
and then he asked me to assist him
in the kitchen: 'Who can digest Melancthon
and Luther, and who likes tripe as old
as martyrdom?' I knew the voice, part love,
part niggling courtier, and I thought
shall I never escape my husband's wars,
his stormclouds in the organ-loft, the knock
which means a visitor who might present
himself as psychopomp or onion-seller?
The sun is up, there's madness at the door,
prepared to haggle—I feel my heart
fly from its anchored place into the sky,
amazed by sunbursts, by curricula
of angels calling out the odds, by domes
of the celestial pavilion, and my family
isn't with me where the palms give shade
to Jesus and in strictest canon voices
sweeten time with just a tincture of
chromaticism. My husband's pupil draws
the stops, Sesquialtera and Principal,
and squirts his diapason down the aisle—
my tears dry and nothing gives alarm
except the tinny echo of my voice,
a cantus left on earth, prehistory to
the lands of Paradise, and no one now
will save my children from the dread of death.

From THE TIVERTON BOOK OF THE DEAD

At the turning of the colour of the leaves,
    Beloved Soul,
When in spite of frost the spider weaves
    A living coal
From its stomach so life may eat from death,
    You must venture
Out of the collapsed flesh and unpumped breath
    In rhyming censure
Of your last state of existence, pause
    To say goodbye
To the bloodstream of your hand and the claws
    Clamped in your eye
And enter the second plane of your ascent
    To Harvest Home
Which is neither classical fear nor bleak enlightenment
    But the great comb
Of everything that is raking perpetually through
    What wishes to be.
The land, its byres and bitumen is you—
    You are the sea
Which strangles waves on a whimsical rock,
    You must contrive
To fall with the gulls and their shit, restock
    The once alive
Air with its terraced applauders,
    Set the high bells
Stirring along the county's unstrung borders,
    Order the shells
Recall the coiled sea into their ears again,
    Face the whitening
Bones of your begetters, harmless and plain
    As sheet lightening,
With the order of their apostolate,
    Clean as a knife
Cut through the blackened and immensurate
    Mystery of life
To the consummation of death, a light
    Of stilled eyes
Like a congress of winds sitting by night
    Till graveyard sunrise.

There is not enough daring in the world
    Or in our books,
Nor in the poet's hope, his conventional pearled
    Epithets, the looks
He gives to pious myrtle and druidical sun—
    We must get a price
For our dying, this process just begun,
    An absurd device
No one believes in but which all are subject to—
    The lords of change
Destroy our flesh to feed us with the clue,
    What to arrange:
Not thing on thing made permanent in hell
    But here in Devon
Like Ursula, determined she would dwell
    In her own Heaven,
Saying to God, 'Eleven thousand virgins,
    Not one more or less',
From whose bright martyrdom there burgeons
    A painterly Princess
In glory, and a wharf where blood drips gold—
    Thus it is, dear
Soul, that after death you wish to be told
    The true name of fear
And God's lost numerals in which he sets
    His feet on earth
With the first radiance, the pristine regrets
    Of life before birth.

WHAT DO WOMBATS WANT?

On the Great Day of Division
when the swimmers swam and the womblers wombed
The Lord was already laying down his rules
to help psychiatrists.
          Before the cloud could clear
and language fit for by-laws straighten
itself out, we had the Super-Real
for lunch and all our happy needs could keep
in touch by touch, leaving words to rocket up
like Sickert's circus-folk. Oh how ready
were the prepositions then to join the gang
of show-off verbs, how innocent as dogs
sniffing at genitalia each adverb
not required to be accountable!
Language was all lift, from ballads to
soft burblings in the bassinette, and said
what critics think—it's onomatopoeia
all the way: the coach is leaving for Aeolia,
the team is singing out its heart.
                    Long since however
we've woken with a hangover and found
our words as serious as any modern student,
the pert rococo jokes and mock façades
which hide our sexiness changed by decree
to insignia on security vans—and who
could doubt that categories mean just what
they say? Our caring doctors are as young
as our policemen, the patient sits in rooms
of chosen shades and hears the laughter from
a Game Show while his noose of terms draws tight.
Even those great savers dressed in light
on TV screens, smiling calmly as
another rare and half-blind creature
passes the safe thousand mark, have dark
inquisitorial urges, shouting in
exasperation, 'What Do Wombats Want?'
                    Therefore we hug
the pure exceptions, denizens of grieving
glades whose natures are not ruled by

trained interrogation, the ones whose names
have launched a blessing on them. Who, if called
Donatus Katkus, could be anything
but a viola player? These become
our heroes and compel our hearts to beat
apace when high despair appears dressed
in its official verbals, when we read
'Workers rally to a Queen of glass
treated with the proper pheromones . . .'
       Back in the jungle
Surrealist feasts continue, sponsored by
the best environmentalists—these things
may yet be doomed but all around them Nature
flaunts its platitudes and quail and gerbil
never ask their Shrinks for an interpretation
closer to the classic. What are we left with?
The doorstop snake widowed from its house,
the china finch, the pencil-sharpener snail,
the banzai good-luck cat—it's no surprise
that what a crowded planet likes to love
is its intransigence, the wastefulness
which lies beyond morality, whose life
is never Puritanical though high
on disapproval. Somewhere in all of us
the riskiness resides, the link to sounds
of love and hate, so like whatever made the grade
before the Lord set out his options—thus
as we prepare to stroke a furry friend
who's brushing by our feet, we dare to hope
even so very late that we'll be lucky
underneath the tree of life, not good.

THE ARTIST'S DONKEY

The Lord giveth and the Lord taketh away!
At the moment he's offered this barrel of a barn
dedicated to a dimbo saint and I'm
to paint it. Today I'd rather settle down
and write a monologue of crunchy poetry
(or lump of prose if you prefer) than fret
in fresco. Good-boy acrylic knows to wait.

When they painted like the movies—Apocalypse
with half a hundred Supermans above
a sea of bums—they always put their friends in
and sought a shine might please or petrify
some dicey Pope. I leave the cave of dreams
to pace a polystyrene altar-front
like Luca at the wall. The word's made flesh.

It's best to see yourself a chef, dressed
for the fire, belly hanging out above
the restraining belt, with not a fresh-washed ladle
on the bench. You have to go by metaphor
till paintings cook the world—a green sauce
for unctuous Eden, a peppered steak when Herod
lets his taste buds flay the banqueting.

Holman Hunt had half a dozen goats killed under him—
the great age of seriousness! My borrowed donkey's
grazing in the yard. He looks as if he knows
I'm putting off the task. My *Flight into Egypt*
may hail a punning plane and he can go
on hold, but when the buzzing in my eyes
subsides I need the creature-calm he brings.

Imagine those in Heaven painting us—
their backward fancy, good Orpheans all,
is limning what they left behind: grace, lust,
uncertainty, as words and sounds and shades
hobble on as many legs as work
back to the Vale of Tears: we come, my Brother Ass
and I and all the Is who fit into a face.

LISTENING TO LEOPARDI

Who is this speaking to you?
Just some dusty spirit,
a bibliophile's 'Gespenst'
(those Northern armies brought
their barbarous language with them),
a warning from the tower
there are too many books
already in the world.

I was a healthy boy
until I crept into my father's library—
I became the ghost of sickness;
from my bowed back imagination
shot an arrow at the world:
for what? My countrymen
still stew in their ridiculous
mellifluous tongue—when was there ever
either sense or poetry in Italy?

Yes, I know of Borges,
all art being simultaneous,
another library Caesar—
but look here on my balance:
one pan, a moon, a village after storms,
wild broom, a dozen perfect poems—
the other pan, provincial boyhood
(even if a palace), death in Naples
(once a royal city) and cobwebs in between,
oh, and some prescriptive pensées
with thick Italy looking up at me.
If it isn't in your head it isn't art,
there are no libraries in Heaven.

What would a scholar want with love?
To write about it? Do without it?
We're a multicultural lot in Italy now,
so *fango* has to rhyme with *mango*.
And all the rhymes are riddling in my head
and all the everything there is
which I pronounced was vanity
goes on being vain in poetry.

THE BLOND ARM OF COINCIDENCE

The scene is Venice, the streets as crowded as
A Browning poem, with confirming details such
As spider crabs in plastic tubs awaiting
Their apotheosis in a *vongole*,
Blue-suited businessmen downing a quick
Prosecco in bars sans stools or chairs,
Tourists galore you know look just like you
And the Piazza's pigeons pecking underfoot.
I meet my old friend William Dunlop
Unexpectedly, crowding through a calle
Near San Marco: unexpectedly,
Since two days previously we'd spent some happy
Hours conversing in a restaurant
And didn't plan to meet again until
I left for Florence. 'You're a dangerous man
To talk to' are his words immediately
To me. 'Why?' I ask. 'Do you recall
Discussing William Empson and Ralph Kirkpatrick
Over lunch? Not together, but both came up
In conversation, and you talked a lot
About each of them. Well, both died overnight,
The radio reported—Empson in England,
Kirkpatrick in America.' I am horrified,
I'm not superstitious usually,
It's just that suddenly creation seems
A throttling mesh of interactions
With gloating gods encroaching on its ends
And fleshless angels leering in through space.
'Willie, I'm sure we need a drink,' I say.
He tells me I should think of it as rational
Coincidence. There's no *mal'occhio*,
God isn't listening. We walk back to
His rented flat in the Castello where
We talk of divas and his PhD,
His sabbatical on 'Shakespeare as Opera',
Not 'Shakespeare in Opera' or 'Operas
Based on Shakespeare'. We don't meet again
For several years. I still read Empson happily
And listen to Kirkpatrick's records of

Scarlatti, consult his book and try to use
The Ks and not the Longo numbers. What is
The meaning of my title? Just that the girl
Who served us in the bar that time had long
Gold tresses and blond hairs along her arms
Glistening as she passed our drinks to us.

WINCKELMANN AT THE HARBOURSIDE

I tell the man
standing by his sloop
we come down from the North
to get away from hope

Water oils around its keel—
to spit into the wake
won't change anything,
what's classic
is repetitively new

History, from Herodotus
to the boy at the *Pensione Mercurio*
is infinite desire
mocked by timeless need

BERENSON SPOTS A LOTTO

It takes me back to my beleaguered youth,
Chiming across an Italy where carts
Rocked down dirt roads and crones without a tooth
Unlocked the doors of chapels, and bleeding hearts
On banners, flung aside, revealed an altarpiece
Whose dim and long-dead donor thought to win
A sort of immortality, his Fleece
Of Gold in Heaven, sitting painted in
A flock Annunciation or some ghetto
Holy Family. Year after year I roamed
The provinces from Como to Loreto,
But this was just the fieldwork: I had homed
In on the big boys from the start and knew
That not just railway magnates but the scholars
Wanted certainties, the only true
Account of Europe, and beyond the dollars
A secret map of Christianity
Waited projection by a doubting Jew.
So these my lonely forays were for me
And for my conscience: I felt the world askew
But told it straight: as Burckhardt was the first
To show, the art of Europe's a crusade
And universal culture is a thirst
In conquerors whose vanities have made
Our palaces and charnel houses grow—
The story must be written, heroes found,
Masaccio, Piero, Michelangelo,
A triumph set to pass its native ground
And bear the Western spirit into space,
With me its true evangelist, the one
Who'll say authoritatively a face
Is duly a Farnese, but not shun
The central mystery, the major-key
Colossi, men whose grandeur connoisseurs
Can only blink at—thus it falls to me
To play commander, wear the holy spurs.
And, yes, you've heard my word's corrupt, my voice
In grading minor masters built my villa,
And somebody has rhymed me à la Joyce,
A prophet, *Teste David cum Sibylla.*

I'm the greatest art expert the world's ever seen,
I make attributions for Joseph Duveen,
From tycoons and bankers I draw a fat fee,
So here's to Vecelli and Buonarroti.
The grandeur falls away and Duveen's dead,
And Europe sinks once more into Avernus.
It's good in one's old age to leave one's bed
And young again to stalk such joys as burn us,
The glorious anarchy of what we love,
All stupid scales of value tossed aside
So that a Dosso Dossi seems above
A Titian and we'd die to prove our pride
In Credi or Melozzo: exhausted now
With rugs about my knees, in a wheelchair,
On this my final pilgrimage, I vow
To praise the greatness of that inner air
Which blows about the spirit: they said I'd find
The cutest Visitation in this glum
And barrel-chested church, so, wined and dined,
I'm here and have to laugh—it seems I've come
Full circle to the proving-ground of youth:
I'm bang in front of something I adored
When as a thrusting expert seeking truth
I first encountered it: the Virgin bored,
The Baptist's mother a strange shaft of blue
And two dogs fighting round their feet, the limbs
Half spastic but in everything a hue
Collated from the spectrum's antonyms—
Lorenzo Lotto, my first darling, I
Assigned you half a page in my big book
But more than ten years seeking-out—are we
Then reconciled—you with your beaky look,
Your death's pre-echo and me at the gates
Of terror and oblivion? Your luck
Was to be provincial in the Papal States,
Not smart enough for Venice where they suck
Up gold from mud and splash it on the stars—
You worked a density that fashion loathed
And paid the price of it, your avatars
The quirky poses, matrons overclothed
And cats astounded by angelic draughts.

Old friend, I'm with you now, I've done with fame
If never quite with money—Arts and Crafts
I leave to Night School mumblers and the same
For those grand galleries and owners—let
Them examine sizes, pigments, drapes, x-rays,
I'll give a provenance in a minute
They won't unseat—and Lotto, our last days
Can be the sweetest; you in the warm wind
From the Adriatic fixing the bizarre
With daily habits; me, more sinning than sinned
Against, and princely in a chauffered car,
Doing my lap of honour coast to coast,
Detesting Modern Art, unpenitent
Of theft or fraud, the last admiring ghost
Of Europe's genius, all passion spent.

CARRY HIS WATER TO THE WISE WOMAN

At the age when any pair of us
wonders who will go to the other's funeral,
to write extended poems where dull fact
is milked of its significance
is the terrible temptation.
Your bank card number, why you're snubbed
by taxis with their lights on, a nail-
clipping in a muesli bowl—something
is trying to get in touch, even if it's only
that now-forgotten dream's prognostication.
You might attempt a definition of unease,
a way to misinterpret Ruskin—
good ideas have little conscience
about the minds to which they will
entrust themselves: there is even an oboe phrase
of winsome beauty in the *Purgatorio*
of Liszt—and so since Pandemonium
the Devil's share of tunes has made
soft afternoons in Heaven something more
than La Grande Jatte with bandsmen
brushed by spittle. What's not expected
is any sort of timetable for this
or theory of interpretation.
We know it's better not to know
our hour of death but have a penchant
for the handier reminders: we go
to plays where youthful love is decked in
lavish packs of flesh, and wise retainers
mouth the nasty things they've kept in store
for sulks and spoilsports. Precedence
crowds the table when my granddaughter
says suddenly, 'No carrots!', an un-
equivocal insistence like the sun;
the world becomes more manageable and death
and vanity late versions of an institutional
pastoral. Martha, my gratitude,
you are my brief redeemer. Nothing can
be known beyond the instruments which measure it
and in such proud reports, as well as stuttering
by numbers, the graves and witches of a tortured

West confess. I must be simple—yes, I plan
to live forever, ripe, as they say of plums,
for picking. All those funerals I've kept
my dark suit for, plus the need to wear a tie:
I've promised to take both granddaughters down
to Glyndebourne in the year 2009—
bless me then you omens and you oracles
and keep the postman walking past my door.

DEATH'S DOOR

I'll have to make it harder, is my thought
    Appropriate to this last decade of
    A century which even old Kutusov,
Cunctator of scorched earth and starving fort,
Could hardly dignify by slow retort—
    Despair I think should shade my attic cough.

For I am using Browning's patent stanza,
    But not to tell a story as he did,
    His curious but circumstantial grid
On which he hung a strange extravaganza
Of narrative wide-ranging as a panzer,
    A cross between *King Lear* and *El Cid*.

No, my intent is to dredge memory
    Of those embarrassments I hope will show
    The turbulence pure spirits undergo
When launched against their will on a dead sea
Of circumstance: here childhood entropy
    Joins hands with geriatric afterglow.

We can't believe that life's a pilgrimage
    To nothingness, that moral monsters stand
    Along the dark backwaters of the land
And tempt us like drunks on a window-ledge
To self-destruction as our privilege,
    God's world before us, His hand in our hand.

'There is no God' and 'God is our Defender'
    Are two precise unprovable decrees:
    A supplicant or a campaigner sees
The same hard option and will cry 'Delenda
Est' or 'Love is such a sweet surrender'
    Inside his tank or falling to his knees.

If all paths take us to the grave, then why
　　Not choose the path of glory; that at least
　　Enjoys some dedication—sage and priest
May be outmoded but you still might try
As tycoon, mediator, super-spy
　　To join Top Table for the Final Feast.

And yet our bodies tell us that the *cena*
　　Will be the same for everybody—not in
　　Its terror or serenity, forgotten
Faith or everlasting love, but vainer
Hopes, a metaphysics stormed by saner
　　Fact: the soul is filed away in cotton.

Or rises in a Zoroastrian draught
　　Through council chimneys while a little dust
　　Put in a box rejoins the earth's soft crust.
Why make a fuss, the swallows ask, their craft
The whiling of the world, an overstaffed
　　Theme Park, like Euro-Disney going bust.

The seeming misery is to do without
　　A meaning to existence, but the child
　　Though born to fear might still not be beguiled
By what his veteran instructors shout—
A system with high precedence and clout
　　But showing murder in the way it's styled.

He lacks the will to pit himself against
　　A seasoned state with his apprentice No;
　　Before him integers and pundits go,
He sees a place that's arrogantly fenced,
Apportioned stupidly, obscurely tensed,
　　Its progress A to B, mere to and fro.

Where can he seek the sign who has to die
　　Unhallowed by the work he's here to do?
　　He cannot own the world he's summoned to
Or rent it at a human rate; he'll try
To lift his aspiration to the sky
　　And in the black of dreams discern some blue.

And that is when he's first brought to the door,
   A portage plain enough, no fancy locks
   Or gilded handles, and just as he knocks
A squirt of music fountains up before
The stroke, there's tears and moonlight on the floor;
   He makes no sound tiptoeing in his socks.

He trusts the cunning of his dreams; behind
   This door is everything there is and nothing,
   So it will never open and he's bluffing
When he lifts the knocker—he's resigned
To being something someone else designed,
   A serious doll made comic by its stuffing.

You cannot quarrel with this door: it stands
   As birth-gift to each complicated brain—
   But what you can do rather than explain
Your choked resentment is to watch your hands
As they plan empires, issue hot commands
   And find an alibi for any pain.

Then voices come which give the door a name—
   There's love, invention, curiosity,
   Truth, evolution, God, eternity—
Some tall abstractions keep it in its frame,
Through each allegiance it will seem the same,
   Roads lead to Rome, all vistas show the sea.

As children and as almost ghosts we glare
   Like Bluebeard's wife at what excludes our gaze.
   It might swing open at one magic phrase,
It might show Blake's hydrolysis of air,
A Paradise we make by being there,
   Justification startled by God's ways.

This door, like some crazed Tardis, will appear
   At certain moments when all else seems bright:
   Not just in cold epiphanies of night
But when the flesh is picknicking and fear
Has donned Rossinian motley with the beer—
   A Casa Santa, it moves at speed of light.

Arcane explainers hasten to its side,
   It lights up like a cinema organ's desk
   For *danse macabre* or *graveyard humoresque*:
No matter what philosophers provide
It stays the one impassable divide
   Between the paradisal and grotesque.

Thus given that we need a Paradise,
   To prove it we've proclaimed this ritual door;
   Our minds which live on time can now explore
Pre-emptings of reward and in a trice
Move up to bonding from the merely nice,
   Once having tasted love hunger for more.

And with no evidence say love is real
   Though fear like Fafner keep the iron gate
   (The hour you knock at will be called your fate!)
Love's what you want to do and think you feel,
Love's voice is music but its touch is steel
   And death not Venus may be your blind date.

You wait for her outside; you're carrying flowers,
   Those garden innocents which symbolize
   A world before the watershed of lies,
But these she spurns, she's after other dowers,
The Dance of Company and not of Hours,
   A house this entrance can't epitomize.

I'm trying, as you see, to change the rules,
   Reverse the major symbols of the trade—
   I've posed a door which opens inwards, made
An inner space, a torturer's school of schools,
More Funeral Gondola than Ship of Fools,
   The gravedigger's and not the gardener's spade.

The door leads out of Eden, not back in;
   It only swings one way. How then did we
   Arrive at this auspicious garden, Tree
Of Knowledge waiting for us, Fruit of Sin
Et cetera? Philosophies begin
   As Browning wrote in Natural History.

This happened on an island—Caliban,
  Borrowed from Shakespeare, had a distant God
  He took in with his mother's milk, his quod
Erat demonstrandum, and like Man
Equipped with capitals, Millennial Plan
  And conscience, knew Him by His chastening rod.

As much as Caliban we must accept
  Existence as an axiom; we come
  Out of the dark and go back where we're from—
But where is that? The keeper and the kept
Are both conspirators; the spark that leapt
  The Sistine ceiling struck its watcher dumb.

Which did not stop the myths from piling up.
  The end of life must be triumphalist;
  Transfiguration, yelling, will insist
You taste the garden agony and cup,
Blaspheme like Don Giovanni as you sup
  With fiends to get on God's guest list.

The island and the garden are just two
  Of our grand venues. Take the many wars—
  St Michael and the Dragon, The Rebel Cause,
The Raptors' Ten Year Siege, The War of Cru-
soe's Ear, Marx's Millennia, The Glue-
  Pot of the trenches—famed for opening doors

On death and on its catalogue of stories!
  Who gains the most—the Church with its cold hope
  Of discipline descending from the Pope,
The artists poised to paint and sing the glories
Of their rulers, or crooks, from Whigs and Tories
  To Republicans, modelled in soft soap.

At least beyond this door the imagery
  Will not be taken from the grisly bits
  Of our decay. A paradox—the fits
And starts of terror stop this side—to see
On fresco'd walls ecstatic devilry
  With forks and irons toasting bums and tits

Is hardly frightening today. Our hells
  Are in Old People's Homes and high-rise wards
  With surgeon's scalpels for King Herod's swords,
Our worst incarceration cancer cells—
No reasoned tone or priestly sign dispels
  The loneliness our dying health records.

And our imaginings of Heaven too
  Now need to be updated. The Child's Park
  Where all is play and no one fears the dark,
Cockaigne enskied, The Land of Cloud Cuckoo,
Cold Calvin Hall, predestined to come true—
  We'd swap them all for earthly sounds by Bach.

Perhaps that's it—the door's for listening through!
  Melodia suavissima, a grace
  That's independent of both time and place,
Settles on every Caliban like dew
And whispering love, says 'this is just for you.
  To you alone I show my real face.'

We all must die. After so long a span
  Truisms should be easily understood.
  The world will rail, the evil and the good
Be pictured on the coin of Everyman,
Our Vale of Tears seem just some Five Year Plan,
  Ourselves lost in the heart of a dark wood.

This poem's now as long as Browning's: his
  Courageous spirit's always hovering near
  And in these verbal junketings you hear
(I say immodestly) the worldly fizz
Of his deliberate Anabasis:
  Childe Roland's slughorn sounds out loud and clear.

NOTES ON SOME POEMS

I

16 'The Picture of Little P.P. . . .': see Andrew Marvell's 'The Picture of Little T.C. in a Prospect of Flowers'.

21 'Covent Garden in the Sixties': the opera conducted by Sir Georg Solti was Richard Strauss's *Die Frau ohne Schatten*.

24 'Late in the Day': EPNS: Electro-Plated Nickelled Silver.

25 'Happiness': see George Herbert's poem, 'Virtue'.

26 'Sixes and Sevens': I observed the phenomenon of two storks nesting perilously high on the dome of the church at the University of Alcalá de Henares, outside Madrid.

27 'Estates and Sunshine': see George Herbert's poem, 'The Answer'. The poem is intended as a modern parallel to Herbert's 'cooling by the way'. Somehow, travel becomes the solution, and is cynically celebrated in the famous exchange between Isherwood and Auden as they settled in their train seats on the first leg of their journey to the United States as permanent expatriates in 1939.

28 'Into the Garden with the Wrong Secateurs': the final couplet reproduces two aphorisms collected in Auschwitz by Primo Levi.

30 'Not the Thing Itself but Ideas about It': see Wallace Stevens's late poem, 'Not Ideas about the Thing, but the Thing Itself'.

33 'We "See" His Poems with a Thrilling Freshness': the title is quoted from a poetry review. The poets mentioned are Auden and Stevens.

39 'The Painter of the Present': the castle which Castruccio Castracane, tyrant of Lucca, built near Sarzana on the Ligurian coast, is clearly visible from the autostrada as you drive between Viareggio and La Spezia.

41 'Unsichtbar aber Sehnsuchtsvoll': 'invisible but full of longing'.

45 'Trinacrian Aetna's Flames Ascend Not Higher': see Thomas Weelkes's madrigal, 'Thule the Period of Cosmography':

> Thule, the period of cosmography,
>   Doth vaunt of Hecla whose sulphurious fire
> Doth melt the frozen clime and thaw the sky;
>   Trinacrian Aetna's flames ascend not higher.
> These things seem wondrous, yet more wondrous I,
> Whose heart with fear doth freeze, with love doth fry.

48 'Goes Without Saying': it is reported that Richard Strauss on his deathbed declared that dying was just as he'd composed it in his youthful tone-poem, *Death and Transfiguration*.

55 'Millennial Rococo': archetypal degeneracies and real events are lampooned alike in this poem: approaching the Millennium needs to be deplored as well as noticed.

II

61 'Guano': although clearly fictionalized, the correspondents from whose exchange of letters the first four stanzas are presumed to be extracts, are Sigmund Freud, Dr Ernest Jones, Richard Strauss, and Hugo von Hofmannsthal.

68 'From THE MARIA BARBARA NOTEBOOK': among the most remarkable personal documents which survive from the households of any of the world's creative geniuses is a collection of some fifty or more musical compositions entered in a notebook kept by and for Johann Sebastian Bach's second wife, Anna Magdalena. The material is not all by Bach himself, but includes pieces by his son Carl Philip Emmanuel and arrangements by Carl's elder brother Wilhelm Friedemann—also music by Couperin, Telemann, and Stölzel (the famous song 'Bist du bei mir'). Bach married the twenty-year old Anna Magdalena in 1721, less than a year and a half after the death of his first wife, Maria Barbara, at the early age of 35. His composer sons, W.F. Bach and C.P.E. Bach were the fruit of his union with Maria Barbara. Little is known of her beyond the fact that she was Bach's cousin. No musical notebook of hers has survived, so my poem is an attempt to make good this omission. It should, of course, consist of music, its only words being texts for hymns and songs. The reader is asked to imagine that the poem is an extract from her commonplace book, composed in verse rather than music.

The material is, naturally, treated anachronistically. At the time Maria Barbara died, Friedemann was only ten years old and could hardly have shown any of the signs of alcoholism and unreliability which later caused his ruin. There is no reason to believe that Maria Barbara entertained any premonitions of her death: her demise seems to have been entirely unexpected. But Bach's celebrated concentration on death as the gate to peace does seem to call for an alternative view from someone who preceded him in making its full acquaintance. Because we know so little of Bach's life and feelings outside his compositions, I have felt free to imagine much that is highly unlikely.

71 'From THE TIVERTON BOOK OF THE DEAD': St Ursula, leader of the Eleven Thousand Virgins, martyred on the Rhine in the Dark Ages, was a native of Devon. She and her companions are pictured in many famous paintings. I had in mind both the celebrated series by Carpaccio in the Accademia, Venice, and the beautiful miniature by Memling in Bruges.

76 'Listening to Leopardi': see his famous poem, 'A se stesso'.

80 'Winckelmann at the Harbourside': the great eighteenth-century German classicist and friend of Goethe was murdered in mysterious circumstances in Trieste.

81 'Berenson spots a Lotto': in his younger days, as an energetic art historian, Berenson devoted much hard work to researching the paintings of Lorenzo Lotto, though he allotted little space to the painter when writing his book on Italian Renaissance Art. After the Second World War, Berenson, as an old man, toured many of the sites in Italy and elsewhere in Europe which he had

known in his heyday. He published a journal of his travels just before his death. The interpolated song is parodied from a verse in James Joyce's *Ulysses*. Berenson's suspect relations with the art-dealer Duveen have been much written about.

84 **'Carry His Water to the Wise Woman'**: the title is one of the teases directed at Malvolio in *Twelfth Night*.

86 **'Death's Door'**: by way of homage to Robert Browning. His poems chiefly recalled are 'Caliban Upon Setebos', and 'Childe Roland to the Dark Tower Came', from the second of which my poem derives its stanza form.

OXFORD POETS

Fleur Adcock
Moniza Alvi
Kamau Brathwaite
Joseph Brodsky
Basil Bunting
Daniela Crăsnaru
W. H. Davies
Michael Donaghy
Keith Douglas
D. J. Enright
Roy Fisher
Ida Affleck Graves
Ivor Gurney
David Harsent
Gwen Harwood
Anthony Hecht
Zbigniew Herbert
Thomas Kinsella
Brad Leithauser
Derek Mahon

Jamie McKendrick
Sean O'Brien
Peter Porter
Craig Raine
Zsuzsa Rakovszky
Henry Reed
Christopher Reid
Stephen Romer
Carole Satyamurti
Peter Scupham
Jo Shapcott
Penelope Shuttle
Anne Stevenson
George Szirtes
Grete Tartler
Edward Thomas
Charles Tomlinson
Marina Tsvetaeva
Chris Wallace-Crabbe
Hugo Williams